THE PICNIC

2

For Glenn

THE PICNIC

RUTH BROWN

Ⓐ

Andersen Press · London

The rabbit sat bolt upright, alert and listening. He had
felt the unmistakable rhythm of footsteps – and
footsteps meant humans – and humans meant danger!

He knew what to do. He raised the alarm and dived
for cover –

underground. The animals waited, listening, tense and rigid, frightened by the dreaded sound of footsteps getting nearer and nearer.

Suddenly it all went black. There was instant darkness.
Total panic and confusion reigned.

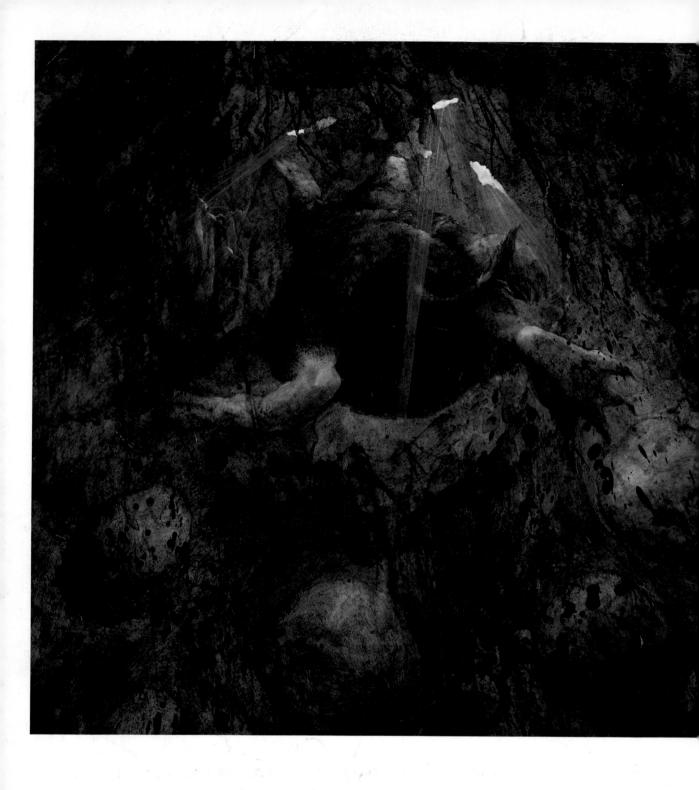

But blind, old Mole, who's used to darkness, carried on his lonely way, tunnelling upwards, pushing, shoving, shovelling clods of earth and clay.

One final heave and he emerged, blinking, into warmth and light. He couldn't see the danger –

– coming straight towards him –

but Mouse could, and was terrified!

He dragged Mole back down into the darkness, bumping,
scraping, bouncing, squealing, dishevelled and undignified,
towards the other animals.

But up ahead there was a new danger. Where there should have been daylight, there was a nose –

– and teeth, and scrabbling claws that tore the earth, flinging them in all directions, and worse – water was rushing in. The animals were trapped between the fangs and flood.

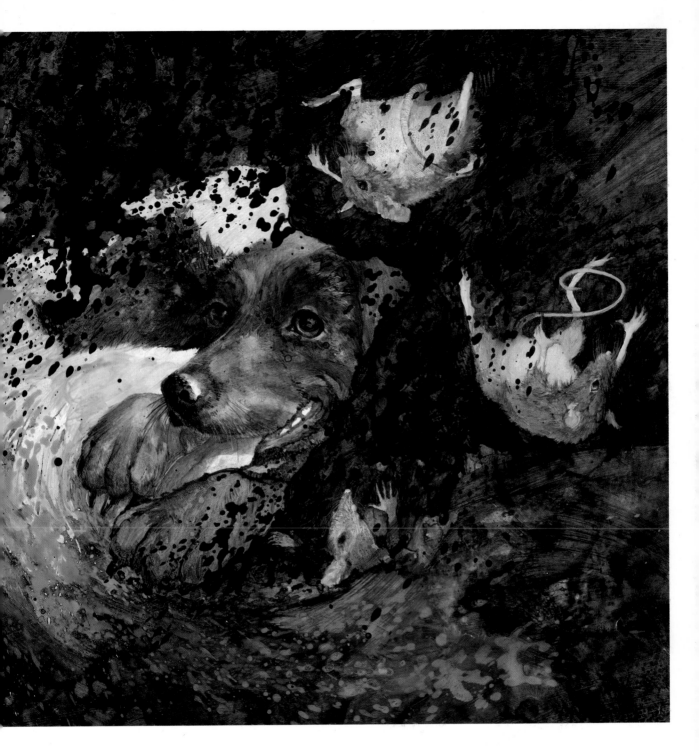

Outside, the dog could chase only one of them; inside, the mud would smother them all.

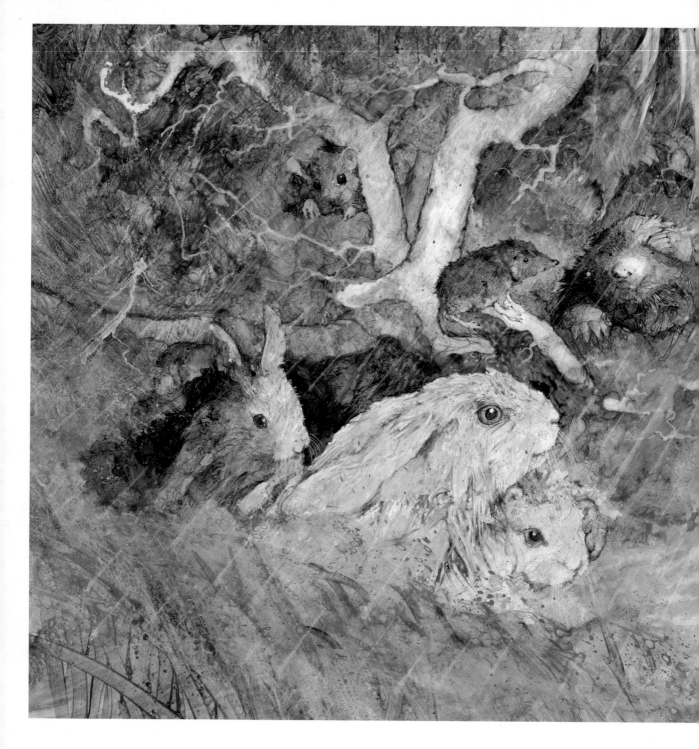

So, desperately, they scrambled out and found that the
dog had fled! Back to his masters, escaping the storm.
They stood in the rain and CHEERED!

Later on they had their own picnic with the scraps of food they found. Then after sunset, dry and sleepy, they returned to safety – underground.

The rights of Ruth Brown to be identified as the author and illustrator of this work have
been asserted by her in accordance with the Copyright, Designs and Patents Act, 1988.
First published in Great Britain in 1992 by Andersen Press Ltd., 20 Vauxhall Bridge Road,
London SW1V 2SA.
This paperback edition first published in 1997 by Andersen Press Ltd.
Published in Australia by Random House Australia Pty., 20 Alfred Street, Milsons Point,
Sydney, NSW 2061. All rights reserved. Colour separated in Switzerland by Photolitho AG,
Offsetreproduktionen, Gossau, Zürich. Printed and bound in Italy by Grafiche AZ, Verona.

10   9   8   7   6   5   4   3   2

British Library Cataloguing in Publication Data available.

ISBN 0 86264 783 5

This book has been printed on acid-free paper